A Rock Solid History of Hawthorne, New Jersey

How stones play a part in this town's history

VERONICA MacDONALD DITKO

Ronnie Monnie Moonie Press

DEDICATION

To Mrs. Laurel Totora (now Mrs. Browning) and Mr. Ron Naylor: If you hadn't encouraged me to express my creative spirit in those formative Middle School years, I would not be where I am today. And to all teachers who naturally inspire and nurture the true people your students are – thank you.

CONTENTS

1 THE EARLY DAYS

Hawthorne may be the place where you live or visit, but did you know that the ground and many things surrounding you tell a story of the land that goes back billions of years?

It is through the science of rocks, **geology**, that you can learn about this history. And what an interesting history it is. The rocks are pretty awesome too.

The land here was formed from volcanoes. But they were not the **cone volcanoes** you see in Hawaii, Japan, or Pompeii, Italy; rather the lava oozed out of **fissures**, or cracks, in the Ramapo Mountains.

Imagine living in a desert about 200 million years ago, with alps rising far to the east and to the west, and small dinosaurs running around, too. That is what Hawthorne looked like.

This large plain would have resembled the Serengeti Desert plain in Kenya. It likely spanned from North Carolina up to Prince Edward Island, Canada, or about 1,500 miles. It may have been even longer than that, geologists think.

All the land in the world was also one big mass at that time, called **Pangaea**. That means Morocco in Africa would have been just a short car ride away.

This area was a dry grassland, since **fossils** of trees have never been found. Fossils are considered rocks too. There was a dry season and wet season with monsoons, which caused heavy rains that flooded the land because it was too dry to absorb it. (**See fossils here from the Goffle Brook in Hawthorne and Duck Pond in Ridgewood!**)

It is in the reddish brown stone and brown **sandstone** rock (also called **arkose** rock) where smaller dinosaurs made their footprints and left their bones behind when they died. This was just the beginning of the evolution of the dinosaurs before they became great, colossal giants.

When people found dinosaur bones way back when, they didn't know what they were. Some thought they were dragons while others thought the bones were just rocks, nothing more.

Many small dinosaurs used to roam Northern New Jersey, such as the **Hadrosaurus (see to the right, photo courtesy of the Library of Congress)**, which had a bill like a duck and powerful hind legs. The Hadrosaurus is the state dinosaur of New Jersey.

Dinosaur tracks from this time period were the size of elephants', but most were smaller, like antelope hoof prints. Dinosaur footprints were revealed recently during construction in the nearby towns of Montclair and Woodland Park. This can happen any time rock ridges are cut to make way for housing.

Later, during the Ice Age, glaciers sailed slowly across the land, moving rocks and forming ridges and valleys. Lafayette Avenue is actually a glacial canyon. Many rocks found in the Goffle Brook, both large and small, were brought here by glaciers long ago.

Hawthorne grew to be part of the first range of the Watchung Mountains. Here, the mountains are mostly **basalt** rock, a reddish-purple rock some say casts a lovely purple glow on summer evenings.

The picture to the left features basalt rocks in the Ashley Heights area of Hawthorne.

2 WHEN HUMANS ARRIVED

New Jersey today is one of the most densely populated states in the country. It wasn't always this way. A few thousand years ago, Native Americans, also called "Indians," mostly from the Lenape tribe, lived in this area. The three clans that lived in the area were the Tappan, Aquakannok, and Achensachys or Hackensack.

How do you pronounce tribal names?
❖ Tappan: [taPAN]
❖ Aquakannok: [aKWAcanick]
❖ Achensachys: [ACKenSACKees]
❖ Hackensack: [HACKinSACK]

Slowly, Europeans came across the Atlantic Ocean in large ships and purchased or took the land from the Indians. These people in Northern New Jersey were mostly from England and The Netherlands. They are also known as the British and the Dutch.

Native Americans lived off the land differently than the Europeans. They lived in a hunting and gathering way. That means they hunted the animals they needed and also gathered food from the land as needed, such as berries and other plants. Indians also moved often to find the foods or water they needed.

Large rocks, such as the Glen Rock at the corner of Doremus Avenue and Rock Road in the nearby town of Glen Rock, were used as landmarks and meeting places to help guide Native Americans from place to place.

A boulder along the Passaic River in the town of Garfield has a bear paw print and a fish. It dates back several hundred years, however some feel it is fake. This **petroglyph** may have helped Native Americans find food.

What is a **petroglyph**? The Greek word "**petra**" means rock, while "**glyphe**" means carving. Put those two words together and you've got "**rock carving**."

Rocks were also used as places of shelter by the Native Americans from rain, snow, and wind. Broken slabs of rock on Garret Mountain in Woodland Park slid down the side of the mountain and created natural tents that the Indians used for shelter. Caves were also like little homes where Indians could camp out.

How do we know Native American's lived here? Well, they left behind many things that are actually rocks. These included **arrowheads** (also called **projectile points**) they sharpened out of rocks and used for many purposes including spearing animals and fish.

About 6,000 projectile points were found by Max Schrabisch in the Passaic River and are now in the Paterson Museum. (**See to the left some of Schrabisch's projectile points in the collection at the Paterson Museum.**) Many pieces of pottery and Indian arrowheads have been found in the Goffle Brook too. A small island next to the Rea Avenue bridge is believed to have been where Native Americans once camped.

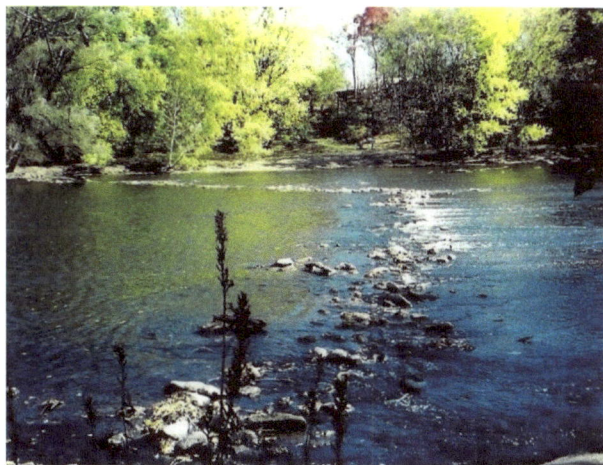

The Lenape also built walls called **fishing weirs** in rivers, which helped them catch fish to eat. There are two in the Passaic River in the town of Fair Lawn, one is between the Fair Lawn Avenue Bridge and Maple Avenue Bridge. The other is across from Fair Lawn Memorial Middle School. (**See above a photo of the weir across from the middle school, courtesy of Tony DeCondo.**)

It is not known if Native Americans built the weirs, or if Europeans copied Native Americans when they built them.

As many as 11 fishing weirs once existed in the Passaic River, but due the building of factories and homes along the river, most of them were destroyed. If you look at an aerial satellite map of the Passaic River in Fair Lawn, you can see the outlines of the two fishing weirs still remaining.

A **wampum** bead factory was thought to have operated on Goffle Hill Road (or possibly Goffle Road by Braen Avenue) by a Dutch family by the name of Stolz near the boundary with Bergen County from about 1700 to 1770.

Wampum beads were made from the white, blue, and purple hearts of the clamshell. These shells probably came from Long Island in New York! Then they were tied onto strings made of native **hemp**, which is a long grass, and woven into belts.

> **Fun Fact:** In 1916, local archaeologist Carl F. Schondorf dug for two months near the factory and found 5,000 wampum beads! They now belong to the Bergen County Historical Society and Paterson Museum.

Wampum was important because it was presented to European settlers like the French and British to help agreements be made, and were re-strung and traded back to Native Americans when European officers wanted to give gifts.

3 FARMERS IN THE DELL

Native Americans did not farm the land in this area. That is a practice Europeans brought with them. It changed the way the landscape looked. Woods were cut down to make way for fields of grain and homesteads. A lot of these homesteads then built mills to sell things like flour.

They used large **granite** stones to grind the grain into flour. The mills were powered by the running waters of the

Goffle Brook or Passaic River. Some of these **mill stones** are now used as trail markers in Eight Acre Woods off of Maitland Avenue today (**see a trail marker above in Eight Acre Woods**). They are thought to have come from the Nicholson File Company in Paterson which dumped debris in the park in

1928 as it was moving to Philadelphia.

Some
notable
mills in
Hawthorne
included the
Ryerson
mills along
Wagaraw
Road,

Hawthorne Mills (pictured above) and Bailey Silk
Company in Ashley Heights on Westervelt Avenue and the
old brick **Excello hosiery-making mill on Forest
Avenue (pictured below**). Some old mills are now
apartments.

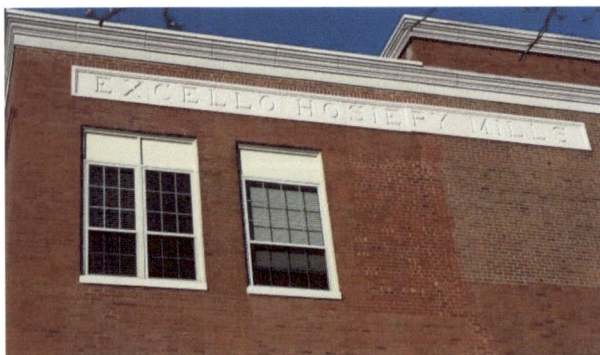

At the end
of the 1600s,
local Native
Americans
agreed to sell
a lot of land.
In 1697, this
land called the
"Wagaraw

Patent" was sold to the Ryerson brothers. They settled here
in 1706.

The "Wagaraw Patent" was 600 acres and began at the
Passaic River, went north up Goffle Road to Diamond
Bridge Avenue, east to Lincoln Avenue, and back down to
the river, making a big square. Some accounts say it even
went up to Goffle Hill Road.

Did you ever notice all the stone walls on Goffle Road? Some of these are very old, and you can tell because they were not cut or formed into a clean shape. They are called **field stones** because the farmers came across them as they tilled their fields.

In 1730, the brothers' ancestor John Francis Ryerson built a house that is now part of Bottagra restaurant on Wagaraw Road. You can still see the large, reddish sandstone that was used to build the house. In 1970, the former owners of the restaurant (the Scordato family) put an addition made of bricks on the old house. Bricks are made from a mixture of clay and other minerals that are baked. Clay is often found near water, like the Passaic River.

The Ryerson-DeGray family cemetery still exists and is located on the Kohler Distributing property on Wagaraw Road (**pictured here**).

All the early families of Hawthorne, which used to be called Manchester, were farmers. If you can imagine, orchards used to line parts of Goffle Hill Road where you see street signs such as Cider Mill Road and Orchard Place. A vineyard that grew grapes for wine existed off of Van Winkle Avenue.

Nearly all of Goffle Brook Park was farms before it became a park in the 1920s and 1930s. Hawthorne also had many horse farms in the late 1800s, and a **bridle path** was outlined in Goffle Brook Park, but never became a true path. Bridle paths are trails just for horse riding. Can you imagine people riding horses through the park?

Another old house in town, the John W. Rea house, sits on Goffle Road, near the Rea Avenue ball field. It is a Dutch vernacular sandstone house and was built in 1840. The stones that were used to build the house were cut by hand. If you look close enough at the large squares of rock, you will see the saw marks left by the men who cut the stone. The bottom of the Rea house into the basement is a different type of rock called basalt. **See**

the saw marks above and a 1933 photo of the Rea House, courtesy of the Library of Congress.

The back of the house was added in 1880. You can tell by the different type of rock and a more modern technique used to cut the stone. Instead of saws, men began to use wire ropes that they pulled from side to side to saw through rock for a cleaner cut. The back side of the house may be removed soon.

John W. Rea was a well-known **minstrel** comedian who was originally from Dublin, Ireland. Rea owned the Christy Minstrels and toured across North America and Europe. His stage name was Jack Raynor. He

> What were **minstrel comedies**? While it's not alright to make fun of different peoples and cultures today, that is what minstrels did. They painted on black faces and did silly things, like a clown. This was something expected back then. But today, it would not be acceptable because doing something silly while acting like a person with a different skin tone is racist and hurtful.

bought the house and farm in 1857 for his wife and children. When he retired from performing in 1875, Rea was elected Justice of the Peace of Manchester, and from then on was called "Squire Rea," and settled small disputes. He also served as Superintendent of Manchester schools.

The Rea House is now owned by Passaic County because it is in the county park. For a time it was rented out to the Riparian Society (which has to do with water rights), Veterans of Foreign Wars, Boys and Girls Club, and senior services for the County.

4 ROCKING OUT

Where did stones to build houses come from? Many came from a **quarry**. There are several old quarries in the area, and some have been filled in to make **condominiums**.

What is a **quarry**? A quarry starts off as a hole in the ground to **excavate**, or dig up, rock. Some get large as the excavation company circles deeper into the hole, around and around like a cone. They use large machines to cut or crush rock, and move the rocks to a warehouse.

The Prospect Park Quarry, which you can see from Hofstra Park, was founded in 1901 by James Sowerbutt. When he died in 1916, his son-in-law, Abraham Vandermande took over and operated it for the next 53 years, until it was sold to Warren Brothers, and then bought by Tilcon.

14

This quarry is basalt rock, and once harvested it is called **trap rock**. It is ground into different sizes and is used in railroad ballasts, the bottoms of septic systems, concrete, and asphalt. **Asphalt** is the material used to make roads and is mixed with a tar-like substance which makes it black.

Special rocks found in the Prospect Park Quarry are now in the Paterson Museum, The Smithsonian Institute in Washington DC, and the American Museum of Natural History in New York City.

Braen Quarry opened in the late 1800s. Then Samuel Braen Inc. began in 1904 to quarry trap rock in Hawthorne. The office was located off of Nelson Avenue. Early workers used sledgehammers and pick-axes to chisel away at rock by hand. It was very hard work. (**See a photo above from Braen Stone from the "Valley of the Rocks" in 1908.**)

Over the years, the company added sand and gravel pits, ready mixed concrete, unmixed concrete and petroleum mixed products. Today, Braen Stone operates plants and quarries in several New Jersey towns.

Another nearby quarry was Upper New Street Quarry

(Burger's Quarry) in Woodland Park which operated from 1893 to 1925. It quarried basalt trap rock.

If you are wondering why you keep hearing about **basalt** rock, well that is because this type of rock is found here. Different kinds of rocks are found in different places. Take a look at the colors in the **geological map of New Jersey (right)** to see how many kinds of rocks are found here.

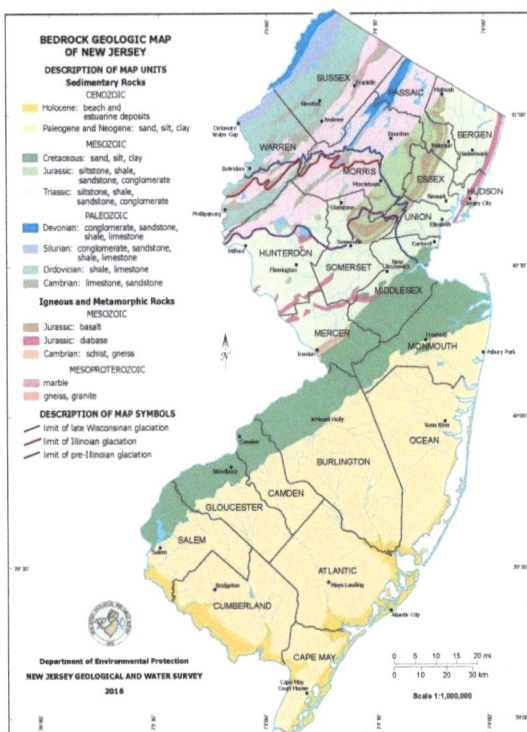

There is one type of rock that is made by animals. These are pearls. Pearls are created when a grain of sand gets stuck in a shelled mollusk such as a clam or mussel. The sand then irritates the mollusk and it puts a protective coating over this grain of sand. Over time, it becomes a beautiful pearl.

Did you know people looked for pearls in the freshwater mussels of the Goffle Brook at one time? It all started with a farmer named David Hower in April of 1857. He went to get mussels for breakfast in the Notch Brook in Paterson. He bit on a very large pearl in one of them.

16

Hower's story led to a pearl rush that spanned the country and even into Canada. People all across this area were scouring freshwater creeks. Some even got lucky.

A rare jet-black pearl was found that May by a servant girl of Mr. Vreeland in Centreville near the Notch Brook. Other pearls were found in Rock Road Brook, a Godwinville creek (now Midland Park) near a rope factory, Signac Brook, Oldham Brook near Paterson, Tuckamuck Brook in Bergen County and waters of Ho-Ho-Kus, Lodi, Suffern, Irvington, Pittstown, and Trenton.

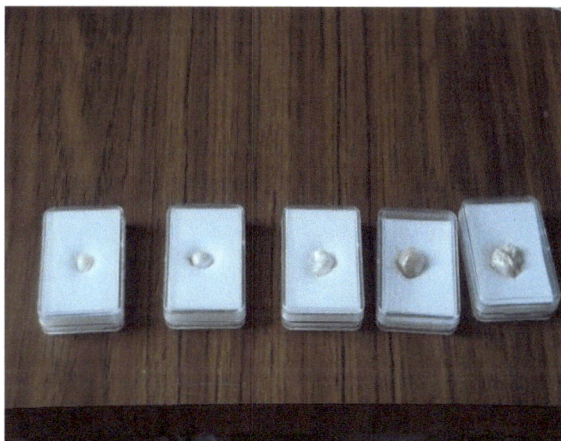

The Paterson Museum owns five pearls from this pearl rush (**see to the left**).

5 IT'S ALL AROUND US!

If you take a walk around town, you will start to notice rocks are in many things. But remember how most of Hawthorne (formerly Manchester) was farms? Well a few things happened to make it more full of houses:

❖ Many people were born around 1888, and more houses were needed.

❖ On March 24, 1898, Hawthorne became a **municipality** (or town) of Passaic County and was no longer called Manchester.

❖ In 1908, developers bought farms to build houses: Arnold Brothers from Elberon to Tuxedo Avenues, Rea Land Company in the north, and Hawthorne Parks Estates Developing Company in the east.

The borough got its first sidewalks in 1911, starting with Rea Avenue. By 1916, most streets had sidewalks, which are made of cement, a mixture of finely milled stones and a binder to glue them together.

Then came paved roads. By 1916, **macadam** roads had replaced most dirt roads. Macadam is three layers of stone with the smallest ones on top that are crushed together. They were named after the inventor, John Loudon McAdam. The macadam roads were designed so water could run off into drains on the sides, rather than collect on the road. Later on tar was mixed into the rocks. This is where the term **"tarmac"** comes from.

By 1900, the population increased from 700 to 2,500. Farms were disappearing. A 1910 **Census** (this is a survey by the U.S. government every 10 years) showed 3,500 people lived in Hawthorne. And houses were trying to catch up. A financial plan from Hawthorne in 1911 showed 4321 building plots were laid out to build 600 houses!

By the end of World War I (WWI) in 1918, the population was more than 5,000 people in Hawthorne. Another population boom led to new houses being built in the 1920s. All these houses needed cement foundations, plaster walls and brick stairs – all made from rocks.

Besides houses, other buildings were being built:

❖ The First National Bank was built in 1925 at the corner of Lafayette and Diamond Bridge Avenues. (**Black and white photo upper right on next page, courtesy of The Passaic County Historical Society, Paterson, NJ**);

❖ In 1925, the **cornerstone** was laid to build a **Masonic Temple** (now medical offices at 484 Lafayette Ave, **photo upper left**);

- ❖ 1931 saw the first permanent building for the town library (**photo lower left**);
- ❖ In 1932, a newly built St. Anthony's Church had its first mass. This church is full of beautiful stonework (**photo lower right**);
- ❖ The Hawthorne theatre opened in 1928. Outside renovations in 2009 revealed a few seascape **reliefs**; and
- ❖ Hawthorne High School was built in 1933 for $500,000.

You may have heard about a harmful stone called **asbestos**. When ground up, asbestos can get into the lungs and eventually cause untreatable lung cancer. Asbestos was used a lot in building materials because it is fire-resistant. Some old roofs, floors, pipe insulators, and shingles today still contain asbestos. An asbestos roofing company owned by R.S. Lanterman operated at 40 Goffle Road in 1916.

Glass is made out of finely ground sand that is then heated up, shaped, molded, and cooled. Schuster & Obert of Hawthorne manufactured glass mirrors on Utter Ave. Many hundreds of houses built around this time also had

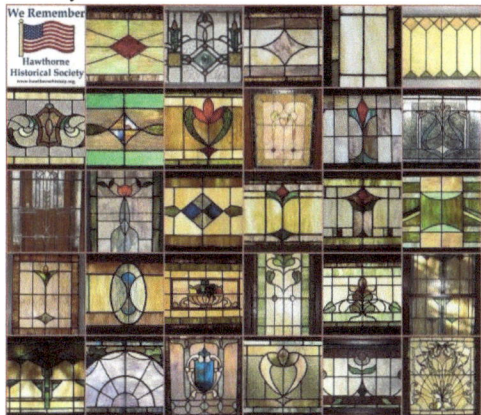

stained glass windows. The artists of these windows are not known, and the manufacturing companies are believed to have been in Paterson. (**The photo to the left are windows in Hawthorne, courtesy of the Hawthorne Historical Society**.)

Around town, some very old houses and buildings have shale shingles on the roof. This is a type of rock.

Other than walking or riding a horse and buggy, people went long distances mostly by train back in the day. Did you know there are two railroads running through Hawthorne? Originally they were called the Erie and New Jersey Western railroads. Today they are called the New Jersey Transit and New York, Susquehanna & Western (NYS&W) Railway.

In 1848, a five-span wooden bridge was built over the Passaic River on the Paterson & Ramapo Railroad between Paterson and Hawthorne. This bridge has since been updated and has stone and cement structures supporting it.

In 1892, trains that used to terminate at Riverside Paterson were extended to North Paterson (this was located in Hawthorne). This caused a building boom in Hawthorne when rail workers moved here, and parts of old farms, such as those owned by John W. Rea and Cornelius Van Winkle, were turned into houses.

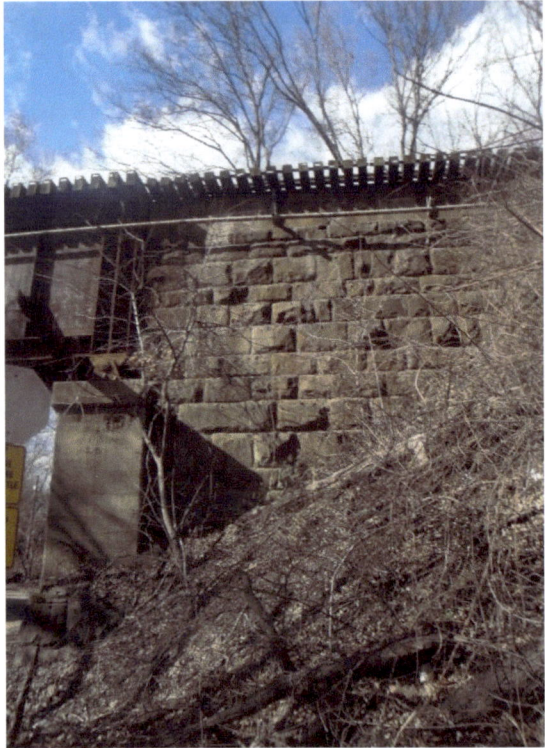

The railroads here were so important that the first sidewalks were created in 1911 to give access to the NY Susquehanna and Western railroads on Rea Avenue and Goffle Road. (**See a photo of a NYS&W railroad bridge above today.**)

Trains also made some everyday things more dangerous. Many accidents occurred on Wagaraw Road where the two railroads came onto one track. First it was horse and buggies, then it was cars. In November 1949, there was a groundbreaking to create the Wagaraw Road grade crossing elimination. This means the ground was dug out below the tracks to make the Wagaraw Road we know today. Large red stone rocks were used to support the tracks above the

road. It was completed in 1951.

Today, you can see many new sidewalk bricks by a very old train station. The Hawthorne, New Jersey NYS&W Railroad Station on Royal Avenue was built around 1900. It used to sit on Diamond Bridge Avenue but was moved back because trucks kept hitting the roof. (**See above a photo at a dedication ceremony in 2011**.)

Where people catch New Jersey Transit trains today off Washington Avenue there used to be a train station about 500 feet down the track by Wagaraw Road. A wooden one was built after the Civil War in 1867 and was moved back at some point when Wagaraw Road was widened.

It was replaced by a small hut in January 1950 that had bricks on the outside, a green roof, and a red cement floor. A man sold tickets at a glass window. It was torn down in the 1970s.

Today, only rain shelters are along the platform for passengers. However, a paved parking lot for 35 vehicles still exists, which was introduced in 1950.

The parking lots, huts, and support structures of bridges all contain rocks! They're everywhere!

Another great place to find stones and history together is in a cemetery. Don't be afraid! You'll learn so much about the people who once lived here.

Hawthorne has a few very old cemeteries up Brock-huizen Lane. The first one you can see is the **Ahavath Joseph Cemetery (see above photo)**. The land was purchased by a group of people from Belarus who moved to Paterson in the 1890s and formed a Jewish congregation called Ahavath Joseph on Godwin Street.

You can tell by reading the gravestones that many people died from **Spanish influenza** (the flu) in 1918 and **diphtheria** in the 1920s. This was before modern

medicine. Some of the stones have **Hebrew** or **Yiddish** words.

Past this cemetery is the **Holland or Vermuden Cemetery (see stone above)** and was used by local Dutch Reformed churches in the 1800s. Now just a few gravestones remain. As you can see, a child only one year and nine months old has a tiny gravestone in the photo. All the gravestones here are written in Dutch.

You can also learn about deceased heroes by looking at the **monuments by Municipal Hall (see one for World War I here**). All these men from Hawthorne served in wars. The plaques honoring them are on these giant and beautiful pieces of stone. A September 11th, 2001 monument is on Goffle Road, as well as a monument for a house that once stood in what is now Goffle Book Park.

6 GET OUT THERE!

Now it's time for you to explore Hawthorne and see all the history that is around us through rocks. Enjoy and never stop learning!

Here are just a few places mentioned in the book:
- ❖ Ahavath Joseph and Holland/Vermuden cemeteries, Brockhuizen Lane
- ❖ Eight Acre Woods, Maitland Avenue
- ❖ First National Bank (formerly), Lafayette and Diamond Bridge Avenues
- ❖ Goffle Brook Park
- ❖ Hawthorne Theatre, 300 Lafayette Avenue
- ❖ Hawthorne High School, 160 Parmalee Avenue
- ❖ Louis Bay 2nd Library, 345 Lafayette Avenue
- ❖ Masonic Temple (formerly), 484 Lafayette Avenue
- ❖ Rea House, 675 Goffle Road
- ❖ St. Anthony's Church, 276 Diamond Bridge Avenue
- ❖ Monuments on Lafayette Avenue and Goffle Road.

7 GLOSSARY

Arkose: reddish and brown sandstone rock where fossils are often found

Arrowhead: this sharpened rock was strapped onto a stick to become a spear or arrow

Asbestos: a stone that when ground up, can get into the lungs and cause cancer

Asphalt: trap rock that has tar added to it to make roads

Basalt: a reddish-purple rock that makes up much of the Watchung Mountains

Bridle path: a path made for riding horses

Census: a survey by the U.S. government every 10 years

Cone volcano: this type of volcano looks like an upside-down ice cream cone and lava can come out of the top

Condominiums: connected living spaces that can either be like apartments or little houses

Cornerstone: when making a building, this stone connects two different walls and often has the date the building was built stamped on it

Diphtheria: this disease is caused by bacteria, makes

breathing difficult, poisons the blood, and can stop the heart, but is very rare today

Excavate: to dig up

Field stones: farmers came across these small stones as they tilled fields

Fishing weir: these stone structures are built in such a way to catch fish to eat

Fissures: cracks in rocks

Fossils: remains of a former living plant or animal

Geology: the science of rocks

Glyphe: the Greek word for carving

Granite: this very hard rock is made of quartz, mica, and feldspar

Hadrosaurus: a small dinosaur that had a duck-like bill and powerful hind legs

Hebrew: this ancient language began in what is now Israel and Palestine by Jewish peoples

Hemp: a long grass that can be woven

Macadam: roads with three layers of stone crushed together and slopes on the sides

Masonic temple: a building made by Freemasons, who are a group of men that help each other and the community

Mill stones: large granite stones used to grind grain into flour

Minstrel comedies: a funny show like a clown that was often not nice to people with darker skin tones

Municipality: a town

Pangea: when all the land on the earth was together in one big mass

Petra: the Greek word for rock

Petroglyph: a rock carving

Projectile Point: this term includes all rocks long ago Native Americans shaped into sharp weapons or knives

Quarry: a place where they cut and take away the rock to sell in different ways

Relief: this is a type of sculpture that is almost three-dimensional (3-D) because it sticks out from a building

Sandstone: it can be different colors and is easier to cut through than other rocks

Spanish influenza: this was a deadly flu virus that circled the world in 1918 and made it very hard to breathe

Tarmac: macadam roads that are mixed with tar

Trap rock: the name of basalt rock once it is harvested from a quarry

Wampum: beads that were made from the white, blue, and purple hearts of clamshells

Yiddish: this language began in Eastern Europe and combines German and Hebrew

8 REFERENCES

50th Anniversary of Hawthorne, New Jersey, 1898-1948. 1948.

Andrews, C.L. 1958. Photo: Erie Railroad Hawthorne Station. Courtesy of New Jersey Midland Railroad Historical Society

Astor, Maggie. 2010, August 21. "Race against time: scientists hope to protect Woodland Park condo project." The Record. http://www.northjersey.com/templates/fdcp?1282828082963 (Accessed August 26, 2010).

Beck, Henry Charlton. 1964. Tales and Towns of Northern New Jersey. Rutgers University Press. Pages 236-241.

Becker, Donald William. 1964. Indian Place Names in New Jersey. Phillips-Campbell Publishing Co., Inc. Page 57.

Belcher, W.H. "Interesting Career of Judge John W. Rea." 1931, September 1. Passaic County Historical Publication, Vol II, No 1. http://www.lambertcastle.org/John_Rea.html (Accessed June 24, 2010).

Bloomberg Business Week. Joel Tanis & Sons, Inc. Snapshot, company overview. http://investing.businessweek.com/research/stocks/private/snapshot.asp?privcap Id=6939795 (Accessed February 16, 2012).

Braen Family Companies. "Welcome to the Braen Family Companies." http://braencompanies.com (Accessed February 16, 2012).

Braen Supply Incorporated. "Get to know us." http://braensupply.com/get-to-know-us.html (Accessed February 21, 2012).

Carlough, Curtis of the New Jersey Midland Railroad Historical Society. 2012, February 22. Interview with Veronica MacDonald Ditko.

City of Clifton and Passaic River Coalition. 2003, May. "Natural Resources Inventory of the City of Clifton, Passaic County, New Jersey."

Clayton, W. Woodford and William Nelson. 1882. "History of Bergen and

Passaic Counties." Philadelphia: Everts & Peck. Page 562.

Clayton, W. Woodford and William Nelson. 1882. History of Bergen & Passaic Counties New Jersey. "Manchester" pages 559-562. Philadelphia: Everts & Peck.

Cook, George H. and John C. Smock. 1874. "NJ Iron Ore & Limestone Districts." Geologic Survey of New Jersey. Mapmaker.rutgers.edu (Accessed May 30, 2012).

County of Passaic. "Goffle Brook Park." http://www.passaiccountynj.org/parkshistorical/parks/gofflebrookpark.htm (Accessed 2009).

Coutros, Evonne. 2012, February 15. "Glen Rock going national: magazine tells boulder's story." The Record. Page L-1.

Cowen, Richard. 2010, December 14. "Call it the rock haul of fame." The Record. Page L-1.

Cunningham, Jennifer. 2010, September 1. "Museum eager for dinosaur remains." The Record. Page L-2.

Dalton, Richard. 1976, June. "Caves of New Jersey." Department of Environmental Protection, New Jersey Geological Survey. Bulletin 70.

DeCondo, Tony. 2008, November 14. Interview with Veronica MacDonald Ditko.

Erie Employee Magazine. 1951. "Looking Down on New Project." May.

Fitzgerald, Elizabeth. June 17, 2008. "More N.J. businesses surviving from generation to generation." http://www.nj.com/business/index.ssf/2008/06/more_nj_businesses_surviving_f.html

Gallagher, William B. 1997. When Dinosaurs Roamed New Jersey. Rutgers University Press.

Green, Jeff. 2013, July 25. "Quarry firm open to depth limit." The Record. Page L-1.

Hagaman, Adaline. 1963. Early New Jersey. The University Publishing Company.

Hawthorne Chamber of Commerce. 1916. Anniversary book.

Hawthorne New Jersey Tercentenary Souvenir Book, 1664-1964. 1964.

Hawthorne News Record. 1924, July 4. "Prepare Plans for Goffle Road walks." Vol 3, No 24.

Hawthorne Press. 2009, June 18. "Theatre getting a facelift."

Hawthorne Press. 1987, July 23. "'Mini-city' draws protests." Pages 1 and 9.

Hawthorne Press. 2012, August 9. "Tilcon Quarry ceasing operation; new developer interested." Page 13.

Hawthorne Water Department, Annual Drinking Water Quality Report, 2011.

Herringshaw, Thomas William. Herringshaw's National Library of American Biography. 1914.

Joel Tanis & Sons, Inc. History. http://www.tanisconcrete.com/history.php (Accessed February 16, 2012).

Kunz, George Frederick and Charles Hugh Stevenson. 1908. The book of the pearl: its history, art, science, and industry. Dover Publications, Inc. Mineola, New York.

Lenik, Edward J. 2009. Making Picture in Stone: American Indian Rock Art of the Northeast. The University of Alabama Press, Tuscaloosa.

Library of Congress. 1933. John W. Rea House, 675 Goffle Road, Hawthorne, Passaic County, NJ. Photos from Survey HABS NJ-178. https://www.loc.gov/resource/hhh.nj0722.photos (Accessed January 13, 2018).

Lucas, Frederic Augustus, 1868 [1904]. Vol 45, Plate LXXIII. Smithsonian Miscellaneous Collections. http://lhldigital.lindahall.org/cdm/singleitem/collection/dino/id/484 (Accessed January 13, 2018).

Lucas, Walter Arndt. 1944. From the Hills to the Hudson: A history of the Paterson and Hudson River Rail Road and its associates, the Paterson and Ramapo, and the Union Railroads. Pages 21, 200-203.

Lucas, Walter. 1949. "Hawthorne Crossing to Go." Erie Railroad Employee Magazine. November.

Lucas, Walter. 1950. "Attractive Hawthorne Station Opened." Erie Railroad Employee Magazine. March.

Mary Delaney Krugman Associates, Inc. "Goffle Brook Park Historic District." 2006. Nomination to the National Register of Historic Places. Prepared for Please Save Our Parkland Committee. Montclair, NJ.

Mason, B. (1960) Trap Rock Minerals of New Jersey.

National Park Service. Historic American Buildings Survey (HABS). 1940. John W. Rea House.

Nehrings, Ginger. 2008, November 4. Interview with Veronica MacDonald Ditko.

Nelson, William. 1901. History of the City of Paterson and the County of Passaic New Jersey. Paterson: The Press Printing and Publishing Co.

New Jersey Department of Environmental Protection. 2016. "Bedrock Geological Map of New Jersey." http://www.state.nj.us/dep/njgs/enviroed/freedwn/psnjmap.pdf (Accessed January 14, 2018).

New Jersey Department of Protection, Historical Preservation Office. 2010, April 1. "New Jersey and National Registers of Historic Places." Page 2. Hawthorne Borough listing.

New Jersey Legislature. 2002. Kid's Page, NJ State Symbols. http://www.njleg.state.nj.us/kids/1024njsym.asp# (Accessed February 13, 2012).

New Jersey Midland Railroad Historical Society, 2012, http://njmidland.railfan.net/ (Accessed February 13, 2012).

New York Times. 1857. August 2. "The New Jersey Pearl Fishery." Vol VII.

New York Times. 1857. July 23. "Markets." Vol VII.

New York Times. 1857. May 8. "New Jersey Clam Pearls." Vol VII.

Pardi, Dr. Richard of William Paterson University. 2010, July 30. Interview with Veronica MacDonald Ditko.

Paterson Daily Guardian. 1857, April 11. "The Pearl Excitement."

Paterson Daily Guardian. 1857. April 15. "Later from the Pearl Fishery."

Paterson Daily Guardian. 1857. April 17. "There are various rumors…"

Paterson Daily Guardian. 1857. April 18. Letters to the editor. "The Pearls found in Bergen County."

Paterson Daily Guardian. 1857. April 20. Local and State Items. "Pearl

Mussels."

Paterson Daily Guardian. 1857. April 22. "The Paterson Guardian says..."

Paterson Daily Guardian. 1857. April 23. Local and State Items. "The Pearl Fisheries."

Paterson Daily Guardian. 1857. April 24. "Searching for Pearls and Found a Diamond."

Paterson Daily Guardian. 1857. April 29. "The Pearl Fishery."

Paterson Daily Guardian. 1857. April 30. "The New Jersey Pearl Fishery."

Paterson Daily Guardian. 1857. July 16. "Pearls at Lawrence."

Paterson Daily Guardian. 1857. June 10. "Pearls at Pittstown."

Paterson Daily Guardian. 1857. June 12. "Pearl Hunting - Interesting Incident."

Paterson Daily Guardian. 1857. June 16. "Pearls in Oswego County, N.Y."

Paterson Daily Guardian. 1857. June 18. "The Pearl Hunters Pitching Pennies."

Paterson Daily Guardian. 1857. June 23. "The Pearl Mania."

Paterson Daily Guardian. 1857. June 4. "More Pearls."

Paterson Daily Guardian. 1857. June 9. "The Pearl Fishery."

Paterson Daily Guardian. 1857. May 1. "From the New York Tribune: The Jersey Pearl Fishery."

Paterson Daily Guardian. 1857. May 16. "More Pearls from the Hohokus Brook."

Paterson Daily Guardian. 1857. May 2. Local and State Items. "Discovery of a Lustrous Jet Black Pearl. Hohokus Pearls."

Paterson Daily Guardian. 1857. May 26. "More Jersey Pearls."

Paterson Daily Guardian. 1857. May 8. "American Pearls."

Paterson Daily Guardian. 1857. May 9. "Pearls."

Paterson Morning Call. 1914, March 25. "Quarry blast injures many." Page 1.

Philip Jaeger. 2008, December 8. Presentation of "The Passaic River: 81 Miles of History" at the Louis Bay 2nd Library, Hawthorne, NJ.

Railroad Avenue Enterprises. 1949. Photo: Erie Railroad Grade Crossing Elimination. October 27. Courtesy of New Jersey Midland Railroad Historical Society

Railroad Avenue Enterprises. 1950. Photo: Erie PA E/B at Hawthorne. January 14. Courtesy of New Jersey Midland Railroad Historical Society.

Railroad Avenue Enterprises. 1950. Photo: Erie Station Looking E/B. January 19. Courtesy of New Jersey Midland Railroad Historical Society.

Rauchfuss, Dr. William H. 1929, November 7. "Funeral Customs of Olden Days." Reprinted in The Castle Genie, Spring 2010, Vol 18, No 1.

Ryerson, Albert Winslow. 1916. The Ryerson Genealogy. Chicago.

Scientific American. 1857. May 30. "More American Pearls." Vol 12, No 38. Page 3.

Skinner, Alanson and Max Schrabisch. 1913. "A Preliminary Report of the Archaeology Survey of the State of New Jersey." Department of Anthropology in the American Museum of Natural History, Clark Wissler, PhD, Curator, under the Direction of the State Geological Survey. Bulletin 9. Trenton, NJ.

Smith, Don Everett. "Images of America: Hawthorne." Arcadia, 2006.

The Hawthorne News. 1930, February 28. "Sidewalks planned for Minerva Avenue."

The Hawthorne News. 1930, June 20. "Erie Railroad Puts Gates at Wagaraw Rd. Crossing." Page 1. Vol 9, No 23.

The Hawthorne News. 1930, May 16. "State Highway Will Make Town 30 Mins. From N.Y." Page 1. Vol 9, No 18.

The Hawthorne News. 1930, November 14. "Cave In Causes Another Delay." Page 2. Vol 9.

The Hawthorne News. 1930, November 17. "State Funds Available for Wagaraw Road Crossing Elimination." Vol 9.

The Hawthorne News. 1930, November 21. "Work Started on Crossing Elimination." Page 1. Vol 9, No 45.

Tilcon. "History of Tilcon." http://www.tilconny.com (Accessed November 2, 2010).

Tilcon. "Prospect Park, New Jersey." http://www.tilconny.com/locations/nj-prosepct-park.htm (Accessed February 16, 2012).

Vermeule, C.C., Geologic Survey of New Jersey. 1900. "Forests of Northern New Jersey." Northeast Sheet. Mapmaker.rutgers.edu (Accessed May 30, 2012).

Widmer, Kemble. 1964. The Geology and Geography of New Jersey. Vol 19, The New Jersey Historical Series. D. Van Nostrand Company, Inc., Princeton, NJ.

Wise Geek. 2012. What is macadam? http://www.wisegeek.com/what-is-macadam.htm (Accessed May 22, 2012).

Zalenski, Annita. 2002. Written in Stone: Gravestone Inscriptions Passaic County, New Jersey.

Zuidema, John. 1946. Photo: NYSW W/B Commuter - Hawthorne, Image 233. October 19. Courtesy of New Jersey Midland Railroad Historical Society.

ACKNOWLEDGMENTS

Many thanks!
I cannot thank enough the many people who imparted their knowledge onto me. They include: Ruth Brooks, Curt Carlough, Tony DeCondo, Jack DeStefano, Heather Garside, Bob Hazekamp Jr., Ginger Nehrings, Joe Osborne, Dr. Richard Pardi, Marty Rittenberg, Norm Rutan, Billy Smith, Ed Smyk, Jackie Walsh, Annita Zalenski, The Hawthorne Press, members of the Hawthorne Historical Society, Passaic County Historical Society, Louis Bay 2nd Library, and the many people of Hawthorne and surrounding towns who indulged my questions and sense of wonder over many years. Thank you to friends Linda Bradler, Ava Caridad, and Katy Leclercq for their talents to make this book look good! And last but not least, I thank my family who spent bits of time without me as I created the pages of this book. This book was inspired by you.

ABOUT THE AUTHOR

Veronica MacDonald Ditko is a lover of history and has written many articles of local interest in New Jersey. Most important to her is sharing this information in compelling language for both adults and children. Her first published book is "A Rock Solid History of Hawthorne, New Jersey" where she illustrates local history for school-aged children through something tangible – rocks. Veronica has also written for newspapers in Massachusetts and New Jersey, as well as mainstream, business, and trade magazines. She is the face behind the longtime "An Accidental Anthropologist" blog in Northern New Jersey where she explored why we do what we do with Seinfeld-esque humor. She is a proud graduate of UMass, Amherst, and wrote for *The Daily Collegian* while at the school and collegiate newsletters while studying abroad at the University of Wales Swansea. Follow Veronica on Facebook at "Veronica MacDonald Ditko, Writer."

www.ingramcontent.com/pod-product-compliance
Lightning Source LLC
Chambersburg PA
CBHW040345060426
42445CB00029B/8